GREAT BATTLES AND SIEGES

LITTLE BIGHORN

PHILIP STEELE

ILLUSTRATIONS BY
RICHARD HOOK

New York

Maxwell Macmillan Canada
Toronto

Maxwell Macmillan International
New York • Oxford • Singapore • Sydney

GREAT BATTLES

First American publication 1992 by New Discovery Books, Macmillan Publishing Company, 866 Third Avenue, New York, NY 10022
Maxwell Macmillan Canada Inc., 1200 Eglington Avenue East, Suite 200, Don Mills, Ontario M3C 3N1

Macmillan Publishing Company is part of the Maxwell Communication Group of Companies.

First published in 1992
in Great Britain by
Wayland (Publishers) Ltd
61 Western Road, Hove
East Sussex BN3 1JD
England
First published in Australia by
The Macmillan Company of Australia Pty Ltd
107 Moray Street, South Melbourne
Victoria 3205, Australia

A ZOË BOOK

Copyright © 1992 Zoe Books Limited

Devised and produced by
Zoe Books Limited
15 Worthy Lane
Winchester
Hampshire SO23 7AB
England

Printed in Belgium
Design: Pardoe Blacker
Picture research: Sarah Staples
Illustrations: Richard Hook

10 9 8 7 6 5 4 3 2 1

Library of Congress Cataloging-in-Publication Data
Steele, Philip.
    Little Bighorn/by Philip Steele.
      p. cm.— (Great battles and sieges)
    Summary: Describes the causes, events, and aftermath of the battle in 1876 between soldiers of the United States army, commanded by General George Armstrong Custer, and Indian warriors of the Cheyenne and Sioux nations.
      ISBN 0-02-786885-0
    1. Little Big Horn, Battle of the, 1876 — Juvenile literature.
    [1. Little Big Horn, Battle of the, 1876.] I. Title. II. Series.
    E83.876.S725   1992
  973.8'2—dc20   91-24065

Photographic acknowledgments

The publishers wish to acknowledge, with thanks, the following photographic sources:

5, 6 Peter Newark's Western Americana; 9 Peter Newark's Western Americana/George Catlin; 10 Peter Newark's Western Americana/Karl Bodmer; 16 Peter Newark's Western Americana/Chief Red Horse; 17t Peter Newark's Western Americana/Robert Lindneux; 17b, 19, 21 Peter Newark's Western Americana; 25 Peter Newark's Western Americana/Edgar S. Paxson; 27 Peter Newark's Western Americana

LITTLE BIGHORN

Contents

73.82
TE

The Little Bighorn River

Montana lies in the far north of the United States, along the border with Canada. The Rocky Mountains, a series of high, snowy ranges, rise in the south and the west of the state. The Bighorn Mountains lead southward into Wyoming, and to the southeast lie the Black Hills of South Dakota and Wyoming. To the east, the states of North and South Dakota are drained by the mighty Missouri River. Here there is **prairie**, or grassland, and the rocky wilderness known as the Badlands.

Wheat and barley are harvested on the grasslands today. Large herds of cattle graze the fields. Two great highways, Interstates 90 and 94, wind across Montana. As drivers hurry westward, they may spare little thought for the past. Soon, however, the towns begin to echo names familiar from history books: Rosebud, Bighorn, and Custer....

▼ *The battlefield of Little Bighorn was known to the Indian warriors as the Valley of Greasy Grass. It lies to the east of the Rockies, in the valley of the Little Bighorn River.*

CANADA

NORTH DAKOTA

UNITED STATES

N

MONTANA

W   E

Yellowstone River

S

Bitterroot Range

Rocky Mountains

Absaroka Range

Bighorn River

Little Bighorn

Powder River

Missouri River

Bighorn Mountains

Black Hills

SOUTH DAKOTA

IDAHO

WYOMING

CANADA

UNITED STATES

Pacific Ocean

Atlantic Ocean

0   100   200   300   400   500   kilometers

0   100   200   300   miles

LITTLE BIGHORN

Memories in the Grass

To the southeast of the city of Billings lie lands reserved for the Northern Cheyenne and the Crow Indians. The Crow **reservation** is crossed by two rivers, the Bighorn and its smaller branch, the Little Bighorn.

A landscape of rough grassland stretches toward the mountains beneath a wide open sky. There are low, bare hills and scattered trees and scrub. There are rocky gullies and dry watercourses.

A grassy rise is fenced off to mark the site where the Battle of Little Bighorn came to a dreadful end. This is sometimes called Custer's Last Stand. Planted spruce trees and white memorial stones mark the places where soldiers died. Today the valley is peaceful. Long grasses blow in the wind.

The Plains Wars

The Battle of Little Bighorn was fought on June 25, 1876, between soldiers of the United States Army and Indian warriors of the Cheyenne and Sioux nations. The American **Plains Wars** lasted from 1854 until 1890. Little Bighorn is one of the most famous battles of those wars, for the U.S. troops, commanded by Lieutenant Colonel George Armstrong Custer, suffered a crushing defeat.

The Battle of Little Bighorn had its roots in a great injustice. The battle produced both cruelty and courage. It also produced great misery and suffering for the Indians' victory was just one act in a longer tragedy.

▲ *Simple stones now mark the spots where Custer's soldiers fell. Carved into the white marble of many stones are the words "Unknown Soldier."*

In 1991, Congress at last agreed that a memorial should be raised to the Indians who died in battle. It also agreed that the National Monument site currently called the Custer Battlefield should change its name to Little Bighorn.

Back into History

Let us travel back in time to the year 1876, only a few generations ago. This is the year in which the telephone was invented. Big cities were growing up around the factories of Europe and in the eastern United States. The European nations were invading Africa, Asia, and Oceania, adding new lands to their growing empires.

The European soldiers were armed with powerful weapons. It was easy for them to conquer people who fought only with spears and arrows. Many of the Europeans believed that this made them more civilized than the other peoples of the world. They were scornful of them, calling them savages. Some North American pioneers viewed the **Native Americans** in the same way.

Indian Lands

The Native Americans were part of an ancient **civilization.** In the Americas they had founded empires and built great cities.

They originally came from Asia, many thousands of years ago. Nobody knows exactly when they arrived in North America, but they were making stone tools in New Mexico about 20,000 years ago. Spanish explorers led by Christopher Columbus reached the Americas in 1492 and, believing they were in Asia, called the people who lived there **Indians**.

As Europeans began to settle the eastern coast, most North American Indians were friendly toward them. However, over the years some of the newcomers cheated the Indians and seized their lands. Wars broke out and many Indians were killed. Others died of diseases such as smallpox, which had been brought in by the settlers.

In 1776 some settlers founded the United States of America. The new country began to buy or settle more Indian **territories** in the South and West. They made agreements with the Indian nations. Most of these **treaties** were soon broken by the newcomers.

The Indians could not understand how land could be "owned" or considered as "property" by humans. The famous chief Crazy Horse (Ta-sunko witko), who fought at Little Bighorn, said, "One does not sell the earth upon which the people walk."

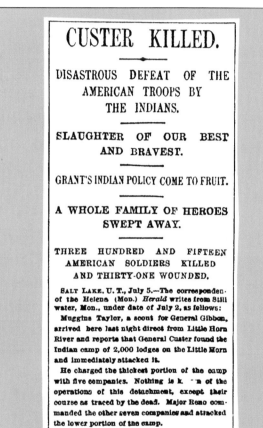

▲ *How do historians find out about past battles? They can visit battlefields and search for clues. They can examine weapons, equipment, or uniforms in museums. Little Bighorn was fought as recently as 1876, so there are also first-hand accounts of the battle. There are official army reports, newspaper stories, drawings, and photographs. There are statements on record from Indians such as Crow King.*

Historians must bear in mind that people do not always tell the truth. Many of the accounts may have been given for political reasons. The accounts may have been retold to make a good story, or wrongly translated from an Indian language.

LITTLE BIGHORN

Greedy for Land

By the 1840s, white settlers were swarming across the Indian lands west of the Mississippi, searching for gold and setting up farms and **ranches**. Indians were again forced away from their traditional homelands. The animals which provided their food and clothing were slaughtered in the thousands by white settlers.

From 1861 to 1865 there was a bitter **civil war** between the northern and southern states. Many thousands of soldiers were killed, including both white and black Americans. The latter were descendants of the Africans who had been enslaved by the first European settlers. After the Civil War many poor whites headed west to seek their fortune. Many had learned how to fight during the war.

▼ *Wagons carrying settlers westward drove across the Indian lands in the 1840s. Some settlers never reached their destination. They were attacked by Indian warriors. United States soldiers were often called in to protect the travelers.*

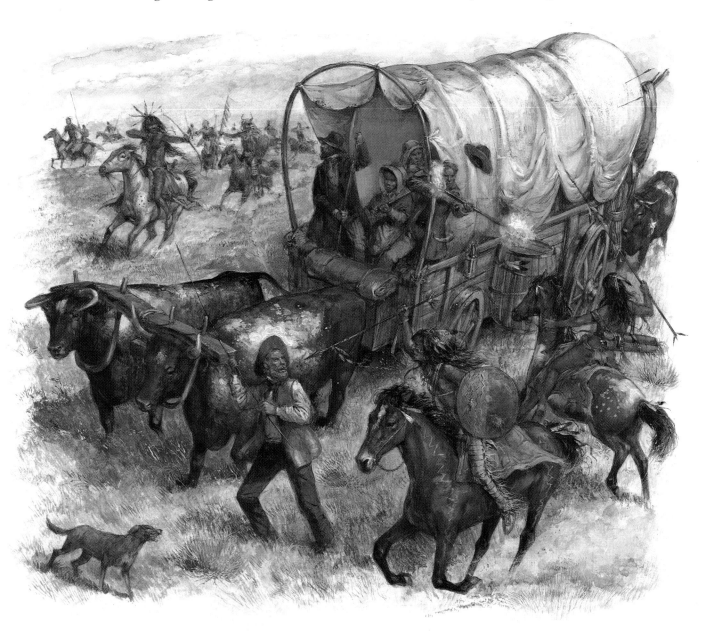

Riders of the Plains

In the middle of the nineteenth century about 225,000 American Indians lived on the plains to the east of the Rocky Mountains. The Indian nations, or **tribes**, were known by nicknames — such as Sioux, Cheyenne, or Crow — given to them by early settlers. The Indians called themselves by their own names. The Sioux, for example, referred to themselves as Otceti Cacowin. The Cheyennes were the Tsistsistas, and the Crows were the Absaroka.

There were many different tribes and smaller groupings, too. Some but not all of the tribes were divided into hunting bands of 100 or more people. Each band was led by a chief and a spiritual leader, or **medicine man**. Decisions about warfare and other important matters were made by a tribal meeting, a **council**.

▼ *The tepee of the Plains Indians was made of tanned buffalo hide laid on wooden poles about 23 feet (7 meters) long. Once erected, it measured about 20 feet (6 meters) from side to side. Flaps provided a door and a vent for smoke. A fire would burn inside the tent. The tepees were pitched in a big circle and could be swiftly dismantled.*

LITTLE BIGHORN

Horses and Buffalo

Many of the Plains Indians had originally lived in the forests to the east. As white settlers displaced some of the eastern tribes, these Indians in turn seized the territory of their traditional enemies. This is what the Ojibwa (Chippewa) did to the Sioux in Minnesota in the nineteenth century. The defeated tribes moved on to the open grasslands. There, they rode horses and hunted the North American bison, or **buffalo**.

In the early 1800s, vast herds of buffalo roamed the plains. The beasts provided the Indians with fresh meat for food, bones and horns for tools, and manure, which was dried for fuel. Buffalo hide was stitched into clothing or laid over a framework of poles to make a tent, known as a **lodge** or **tepee**.

By the end of the century the buffalo was almost extinct. It had been needlessly slaughtered by white hunters. One of these was William Cody, an Army **scout** during the Plains Wars. Buffalo Bill, as he was known, once shot 5,000 buffalo in just 18 months. Without buffalo, the Plains Indians were doomed.

Dances and Visions

Each year the hunting bands would gather with others of their tribe. Tales were told of **skirmishes**, or fights, with other tribes. There were important religious rituals and dances to perform. These often involved chanting and stamping until the performers were exhausted.

The Indians believed in spirits, often in animal form, which looked after them. The spirits could be seen in powerful visions. It was particularly important to find out the meanings of these visions and perform dances when preparing for war. Before the Battle of Little Bighorn, a group of warriors practiced a Dying Dance. They vowed that they would fight in the battle until they died.

▼ *This scene was painted by George Catlin in 1835, when buffalo were still plentiful on the plains. Soon the Indians' hunting grounds were taken over by the white settlers, and the huge herds of buffalo were destroyed. The Indians then had to rely on the government to hand out supplies.*

The Settlers

About 400,000 whites had settled the Great Plains of North America by the 1860s. They had moved into the lands of the Indians, which were not yet a part of the United States. Their numbers grew as the East became more and more crowded and people moved westward.

Many settled as farmers, building sod houses or log cabins. Others were miners, traders, saloon owners, storekeepers, or railroad workers. In 1869 a railroad was completed which linked the eastern states with the West Coast, crossing Indian land.

Forts and Settlements

The army built wooden forts for soldiers who would protect the settlers and travelers. Many of the newcomers joined the army, or at least served for brief periods before **deserting**. Women also found work in the forts, schools, saloons, and stores of the "Wild West."

The settlers came from many different backgrounds. Custer's men included an Irishman, an Italian, a Canadian, a Frenchman, and an African-American. Black troops were known to the Indians as "buffalo soldiers."

The first settlements were rough-and-ready places, where fights were often settled at gunpoint. Most of the settlers were hardworking people who had led tough lives. They knew little about the Indians, except that they were fierce, often cruel, warriors and were not Christians like themselves.

▼ *Wooden forts were built in Indian territory. They provided bases for the U. S. army, which protected settlers, miners, and railroad workers from attack. Treaties were signed at the forts, and food and blankets were given to the Indians. Indian warriors were often imprisoned in them.*

LITTLE BIGHORN

Creating Trouble

There were some settlers who were always ready to stir up trouble. They ignored the government's treaties with the Indians and took every opportunity to cheat them when they traded. In fact, they despised all Indians, seized their land, poisoned their food, and rode through their sacred places.

Exaggerated stories were published by the newspapers, which fanned this **racism**. There were public calls for the complete destruction of all the Indian nations. The Indians could not understand this hatred. They wished to ride freely and to follow their own way of life.

In the eastern cities, many of the whites did have sympathy for the Indians. However, their views were often unrealistic, gained from sentimental poems and romantic adventure stories. These easterners did nothing practical to prevent the seizure of Indian lands. More and more tribes were forced to live in log cabins on reservations, far from their traditional hunting grounds, and deprived of their traditional way of life. Many Indian families were forced to starve, and many died.

▲ *The settlers lived in fear of the Indians. They wished to protect their hard-won possessions and their families from attack.*

On the Warpath

The Plains Indians fought on horseback. They carried out raids, led their enemies into difficult or unfamiliar country, and then ambushed them. They were expert **guerrilla** fighters, avoiding big battles where the army could use cannons against them. Many of the Indians were skilled trackers, able to locate an enemy by examining every hoofprint and blade of grass. Tribes sent messages to each other with **smoke signals**, drums, or flashing mirrors.

War Paint and Bravery

Indian warriors aimed to strike fear into the enemy. In battle, they yelled and screamed. They looked terrifying, smearing their faces with paint made from soil, berries, grease, charcoal, or buffalo blood. Many fought naked or with very few clothes on. Others wore special clothing, decorated with fur, quills, or beads. Some warriors wore hats or uniform jackets taken from soldiers.

The chiefs ordered the warriors into battle but had little control over the fighting. Each warrior had to prove himself with daring deeds, such as touching an enemy's body with a special lance, called a **coup stick**. Some of the young warriors belonged to groups with names such as the Brave Hearts Society. They vowed they would never retreat from the enemy.

Sioux warrior

Cheyenne warrior

◄ *Indian warriors wore the feathers of crows, eagles, and buzzards. Each of these was a kind of badge, which showed how experienced the warrior was. Important warriors wore a long, feathered headdress — a war-bonnet — sometimes decorated with buffalo horns. Feathers might also be attached to small, round shields made of buffalo hide.*

LITTLE BIGHORN

Bows, Arrows, and Guns

The weapons of the Plains Indians varied from one tribe to another. They fought with spears or lances and with knives. Wooden clubs were fitted with stone blades or knives to make **tomahawks**. Many warriors carried iron hatchets or light axes.

Bows were about three feet (one meter) long. They could be reloaded at great speed and were powerful enough to shoot an arrow through a buffalo. Each warrior made his own arrows, which were the length of his arm. They were decorated with tribal markings. The arrowheads were made of razor-sharp stone, sheet iron, or scrap metal. Hunting arrows were designed to be reused. War arrows were designed to be used only once, as the arrowheads were lodged in the victim's body.

The Indians used many kinds of guns, including **carbines** and **revolvers**. They bought firearms from trading posts or seized them from the enemy. Many were supplied by the government itself, which often gave out weapons with other supplies.

Fighting for the Whites

The Indian nations were never united. They had fought each other for hundreds of years. White settlers encouraged one tribe to fight another. They also persuaded tribes to join forces with the U.S. soldiers when fighting their old enemies. For example, the Crow and Shoshone Indians fought with the soldiers against the Sioux and Cheyenne.

Indian warriors were well known for **scalping** their enemies. Like warriors in some other parts of the world, they cut off hair and skin from their victim's head. This practice was encouraged by the whites, who paid Indian **allies** for bringing them the scalps of their enemies. Many U.S. soldiers in the Indian wars also scalped their enemies.

▲ *Scouts were warriors who went ahead of the main fighting force. They tracked down the enemy and watched out for signs of ambush. They were used by both sides.*

The United States Army often used Indian scouts. Why did these warriors agree to serve the whites? They may have been Indians who wished to seek revenge on old enemies or who had quarreled with their own tribe. Many scouts needed the money they were paid by the army.

Soldiers and Weapons

The United States Army units included **infantry** soldiers, who fought on foot, and **cavalry**, or horsemen. Eleven years after the end of the Civil War, many **veterans** from that war were overconfident. They believed that if they had been able to defeat a great army on a modern battlefield, then a few Indians in the hills should be easy to deal with.

They soon learned that this was a different kind of fighting. The Indians seemed to melt into the landscape. Arrows proved to be as deadly as any gunshot. However, the soldiers had many advantages. They could use the trains and steamboats for transportation, and they could use the **telegraph** to send messages.

Many of the troops were new recruits. They barely knew how to fire a gun. When life in the forts was not dangerous, it was dull, and the food was often either moldy or rock hard. Some of the officers were poorly trained, quarrelsome drunkards. In an attempt to keep the soldiers under control, **discipline** was harsh. Some troops deserted or killed themselves. Others died of diseases such as cholera.

◄ *The Indians called them Bluecoats. These cavalry soldiers include a corporal (right) and a first lieutenant (left). The first lieutenant is wearing irregular dress. He carries field glasses for scanning the hills and his own knife in a studded sheath.*

LITTLE BIGHORN

▼ *In the "Wild West," there was no control over the use of guns. Soldiers, settlers, hunters, and Indians all used rifles, handguns, and shotguns.*

Winchester carbine (1866)

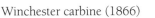

Sheath knife

Colt Single Action Army revolver (1873)

Guns and Swords

Many new and deadly firearms were produced at the time of the Civil War and the Plains Wars. They were used by settlers and soldiers alike. Sometimes these guns overheated and exploded. At Little Bighorn, the soft copper shells often jammed in the guns. Famous types of rifles included the Sharps carbine and the Winchester; the various Colt revolvers were popular handguns.

Large guns, or **artillery**, were also used by the cavalry. Gun carriages were heavy and slow in rough country, but just the deafening noise of the cannon was sometimes enough to turn aside an enemy charge.

Before Little Bighorn, Custer wondered whether to use the Gatling guns that had been brought along. These early machine guns had been used by the army for ten years. They had either six or ten barrels which were turned around by a handle. Custer decided that they would only get in the way and left them back at base camp.

Personal weapons included all kinds of **sheath knives**, which were used in hand-to-hand fighting. Troops were issued cavalry swords, or **sabers**. Few soldiers bothered to take them to Little Bighorn, for they were too clumsy to be used in fast, close fighting.

All Kinds of Uniforms

After the chaos of the Civil War there were problems in supplying the troops with equipment. Uniforms did not fit and boots were in short supply. By the 1870s many of the troops had become used to wearing their own clothes.

The official cavalry uniform was made up of light blue trousers with a yellow stripe down the sides and dark blue jackets or coats. Officers wore black hats with broad brims. The lower ranks wore small caps decorated with badges and the letter of their company. In the field, troops often wore checked or plain shirts and corduroy trousers. At Little Bighorn, Major Marcus Reno went into battle wearing a straw hat. Custer himself wore a fringed buckskin jacket.

Trouble in the Hills

▲ *The Indians recorded the terrible history of these years in small pictures. The warriors gallop by on their ponies; the Bluecoats fire their guns. The Plains Wars were fought with savage cruelty.*

The 1860s were troubled times. In 1864 a force of Colorado militia under Colonel J. M. Chivington attacked a peaceful Cheyenne village camped at Sand Creek, near Fort Lyon, Colorado. One of the camp's leaders, Black Kettle, had been told that as long as he flew the American flag his people would not be harmed.

Ignoring this sign of friendship, the soldiers attacked. They fired on the tepees, even though most of the men were out hunting. Three hundred Indian men, women, and children were killed, and most of these were scalped by the soldiers.

In 1866 soldiers were sent to build forts along the Bozeman Trail, to protect miners traveling to Montana. The soldiers were invading the best hunting grounds of the Plains Indians. All summer long the soldiers were attacked by the Sioux led by Red Cloud. That December the Indians launched a violent attack on Fort Phil Kearny, commanded by Captain William J. Fetterman, and killed every one of the soldiers stationed there.

◄ *Gall was a war chief of the Hunkpapa Sioux. He was born in what is now South Dakota in about 1840. In 1866 he joined other Sioux in the attacks on troops in Montana. He became famous at the Battle of Little Bighorn, and died in 1893.*

The Death of Black Kettle

In 1868 the cavalry was again sent to attack Cheyenne villages. This time, Chief Black Kettle was camped along the Washita River. He was killed and his people were gunned down in the mud. Ninety-two of the dead were old men, women, or children. Only eleven, including the chief, were warriors.

The officer in charge of this terrible slaughter was George Armstrong Custer. He burned the tepees and all the villagers' belongings, and killed about 800 ponies and mules. He reported a great victory to his commanding officer, General Philip Sheridan. Sheridan agreed.

A Way Forward?

In 1868 it seemed that there was at least one piece of good news. The government signed a treaty with the Indians. The treaty "gave" them the Black Hills in the western part of what is now South Dakota. In reality, this area already belonged to them. However, the treaty did make one thing absolutely clear:

> *No white person or persons shall be permitted to settle upon or occupy any portion of the territory, or without the consent of the Indians to pass through the same.*

► *George Armstrong Custer was born in Ohio in 1839. He was well-known for boasting and exaggeration. After the battle at Washita he reported that 103 Indian warriors had been killed. In fact only 11 were dead. Most of the others were women and children.*

The Chief of All Thieves

It was Custer who started the war that was to bring about his own downfall. In 1874 he led an expedition to explore the Black Hills. The expedition numbered 1,200 men and included journalists and **prospectors**. A brass band mounted on white horses played Custer's favorite tunes. On the way, they came across some of the platforms where the Indians had laid out their dead. The soldiers pulled down the graves and stole the dead men's possessions as souvenirs.

What about the treaty? The government had made it absolutely clear that this land belonged to the Sioux. But, by allowing Custer into the Black Hills it was breaking this agreement. The people in the government had thought that the Black Hills were worthless. Now they had changed their minds, for miners claimed to have found gold there. Custer's expedition was sent to find out if these rumors were true.

The Hills Are Not for Sale

There *was* gold. Halfheartedly, the government tried to keep the miners out of the Black Hills. They failed, so in September 1875 they called a meeting with the Indians. More than twenty thousand Sioux turned up, along with Cheyenne and Arapaho Indians. The government offered to buy the Black Hills from them.

▼ *Covered wagons, gun carriages, and long lines of cavalry kick up dust as they head for the Black Hills of South Dakota. To Plains Indians such as the Sioux, Custer's 1874 expedition was not only illegal but an insult to their religious beliefs.*

LITTLE BIGHORN

The Indians refused to sell the hills at any price. They would not allow miners into the territory. After all, the Black Hills, or Paha Sapa, were one of their most holy places. They went there to have visions of the spirit world.

The white men were greedy for gold. They ordered the Sioux to report to reservations. It was a bitter winter that year, with deep snow. Most Indians were simply unable to make the journey. They could not obey the order. In February 1876 the government decided to make war on the Sioux and Cheyennes.

General Sheridan was in command. He ordered Generals George Crook and Alfred Terry to prepare for **campaigns** in the region of Rosebud Creek and the Powder and Bighorn rivers.

George Armstrong Custer

Custer was looking forward to what he hoped would be his last, heroic campaign. Perhaps he could then retire and become a famous politician. He was a conceited man who liked to show off. The Indians called Custer Longhair, because he had long, curly hair. After Custer's expedition to the Black Hills, the Indians had another name for him: The Chief of all Thieves.

At the military academy, West Point, Custer had been at the bottom of the class. However, in the Civil War he became famous for brave cavalry charges at the enemy lines. He became a brigadier general at the age of twenty-three, and was temporarily given the rank of major general. At the time of Little Bighorn, Custer was actually a lieutenant colonel, but he is often known as General because of this temporary rank.

Custer was known to be courageous and a fierce fighter, but sometimes he seemed to be lacking in caution. He fell into furious rages. He believed in harsh discipline and was unpopular with the soldiers and with many other officers.

▼ *Custer makes plans with his Indian scouts. His favorite staghound lies on the grass. Before the Little Bighorn campaign Custer cut off the flowing locks for which he was famous.*

Sitting Bull's Vision

General Crook marched north from Fort Fetterman. On March 17, 1876, some of his troops under Colonel Joseph Reynolds attacked a peaceful Indian camp near the Powder River. Three cavalry units charged the tepees, shooting in all directions. This time most of the Indians escaped, but their village was burned and their horses were stolen. Later, the Indians managed to steal them back again, to the fury of Crook. The war had begun.

▼ *Three columns of troops marched into Montana. They intended to trap the Indians between them, so that none could escape.*

The Advance on Little Bighorn 1876

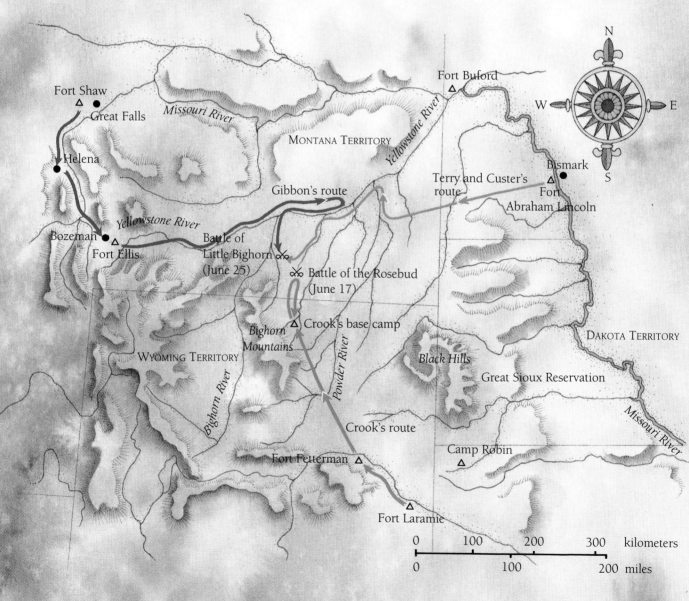

LITTLE BIGHORN

The Sun Dance

That spring, the Indians gathered in larger and larger bands of Cheyennes and Sioux. The Hunkpapa Sioux held a great Sun Dance. This was a dance in which the warriors danced until exhausted. By self-inflicting wounds, their flesh was slashed, poked, and pulled apart. It was very painful. Great bravery was needed, for no signs of fear could be shown. The great warrior and medicine man Sitting Bull (Tatanka-yatanka) took part in the ceremony. He stared at the sun until he collapsed.

When Sitting Bull awoke, he told a warrior called Black Moon that he had had a vision. Bluecoat soldiers were dropping into his camp like grasshoppers. Black Moon explained the dream to the Sioux. The Great Spirit was giving them the white men because they "had no ears." By this, he meant that they refused to listen to reason. War was coming to the white men.

The Battle of the Rosebud

Soon Crook's Bluecoats and Indian scouts were spied in the Rosebud valley. On June 17, Crazy Horse led his Oglala Sioux warriors out to meet them. After furious fighting, the soldiers were forced to retreat. They had lost ten men and the Indians had lost thirty-six.

The Sioux and their allies now moved their camp westward, to the valley of the Little Bighorn. More and more warriors joined them there, quietly slipping away from the reservations. For months they had been hoarding weapons and saving ammunition.

The Three-way Plan

Crook returned south to his base camp. He could do little except wait for **reinforcements**. Crook had arranged for two other armies to close in on the Sioux and Cheyenne encampment.

One army including 450 infantry was heading eastward along the banks of the Yellowstone River. At its head was Colonel John Gibbon, known to the Indians as The One Who Limps. The other army had been ordered to head westward from Fort Abraham Lincoln, on the Missouri River. It was commanded by Generals Terry and Custer.

▲ *Sitting Bull had become one of the most respected Sioux leaders. He was probably born in southern Dakota Territory in the 1830s. Like Custer, he was a vain man and a brave warrior. He was well-known for composing songs. Sitting Bull decided it was time for his people to take a stand against the white men.*

Into the Hornets' Nest

General Custer had said good-bye to his wife Elizabeth on May 17, 1876. It was time for the march westward to the Yellowstone River. Where this river joined Rosebud Creek, the officers met on a steamboat called the *Far West*. There, they drew up their battle plan.

Gibbon and Terry were to join forces and advance down the valley of the Bighorn. Custer would lead the Seventh Cavalry down Rosebud Creek and then turn westward to the Little Bighorn River. Crook's troops would stop the Indians escaping to the south. Nobody knew that Crook had already been forced to retreat.

Custer had once boasted that he could defeat the whole Sioux nation with just one cavalry **regiment**. For this expedition, he had 31 officers, 585 men, and a number of scouts from the Crow and the Arikara (Sahnish) tribes. The unit included his brother-in-law, nephew, and two brothers. A journalist also came along, to write up the story for the newspapers.

▲ *The troops advanced cautiously. Any equipment they dropped would be found by the Indians. In fact, the Indians were soon aware of the Bluecoats. They heard their horses and saw the smoke of their campfires.*

A Growing Fear

The march was hot and dusty. The men took their jackets off and rolled them over the saddles. Custer was impatient to turn west and hurried his troops forward, eager that no other unit should win all the "glory."

His men were becoming anxious. They encountered warning signs such as the tracks of thousands of ponies. The scouts were also afraid. Some had a strange feeling that they would never return. They marched all through the night of June 24, without camping. By noon, the soldiers were approaching the huge Indian camp.

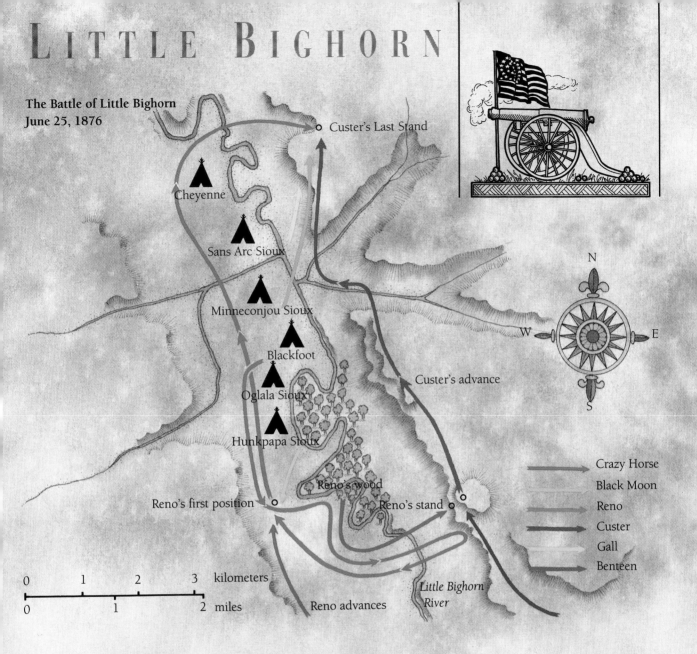

LITTLE BIGHORN

The Battle of Little Bighorn
June 25, 1876

Cheyenne

Sans Arc Sioux

Minneconjou Sioux

Blackfoot

Oglala Sioux

Hunkpapa Sioux

Custer's Last Stand

Custer's advance

Reno's wood

Reno's first position

Reno's stand

Little Bighorn River

Reno advances

→	Crazy Horse
→	Black Moon
→	Reno
→	Custer
→	Gall
→	Benteen

```
0        1        2        3    kilometers
0                 1              2    miles
```

N
W   E
S

Custer ignored all the clues. He did not realize that this was one of the biggest tribal gatherings ever seen in North America. The tepees were arranged in five or six large circles along the Little Bighorn River. There were also temporary shelters of branches, called **wickiups**. Perhaps fifteen thousand Indians were camped there, many of whom were fighting men.

▲ The Indian lodge circles were on the western bank of the Little Bighorn. Reno attacked the southern end of the camp. It was a bad mistake.

Splitting Up

Custer halted the column and ordered the cavalry to divide into four sections. One company of troops was to remain to guard the baggage and ammunition. Captain Frederick Benteen was to take three companies to scout the hills. No Indians were to be allowed to escape.

Major Marcus Reno was to cross the river with three companies and attack the southern end of the camp. Custer was to advance to the east of the river and attack the northern part of the camp. He led five companies, which numbered more than 260 men.

Custer's Last Stand

Reno's soldiers galloped toward the camp, firing at people as they scattered. The wives and children of Gall, the great warrior of the Hunkpapa Sioux, were gunned down. Everywhere the Indians were scrambling for their horses and weapons. Soon swarms of Sioux were attacking Reno. Gall led the charge, in a frenzy of rage.

Reno panicked. His troops dismounted to form a line against the charging Indians. When the survivors remounted, they were pushed eastward to a small wood that stood in a bend of the river. As they took up positions, many were killed.

Crazy Horse's warriors now swarmed in to attack Major Reno's men. Reno retreated again, fleeing from the wood. Those soldiers who managed to cross the river headed for the hills to the east. There, they could defend themselves. They were later joined by Captain Benteen, but had to stay there until Custer's defeat was certain. The fighting was brutal and confused. Some people later accused Reno of being a coward. Others claimed he was drunk. However, after the battle a special court of inquiry cleared him of any misconduct.

Many of the Indians who had been fighting Reno soon crossed back over the river to ride around the camp. They were setting a fatal trap for Custer.

Custer's Mistake

As Custer's **column** advanced, he watched the camp through field glasses. When he saw only women and children, he probably assumed that many of the warriors were out hunting. He moved into an attacking position. Then too late, he realized his mistake. The warriors were actually preparing an ambush.

The Indian charge was deadly. Custer's men were forced back to the high ground and chased northward by Gall and Black Moon. Crazy Horse's warriors streamed across the Little Bighorn from the west, above the Cheyenne lodge circle. Custer was soon surrounded.

The Final Fight

The warriors closed in, wheeling around and around. The soldiers dismounted and fired from behind their dead horses. "I have never seen such brave men," said one Indian later. Fighting was hand-to-hand and desperate. Guns which jammed were thrown to one side. The troops drew their knives in despair. Nobody knows for certain how Custer died. Some say he was shot through the side. Within half an hour it was all over. Every one of Custer's men lay dead.

The battlefield fell silent. The Indians stripped the dead of their clothes and possessions. Many soldiers were scalped. Their bodies were left slashed and cut by the warriors' weapons.

▶ *The final stand made by Custer and his men became famous throughout the world. Heroic paintings showed the general blazing away with his gun. The reality of warfare is always very different. Custer and his men were confused and desperate, and so were their enemies. When the battle ended, about 268 of Custer's men, 6 Cheyennes, and 24 Sioux lay dead. Some soldiers, bloody and dying of thirst, tried to surrender. They were cut down.*

After the Battle

The Indians mourned their dead and laid out the bodies of their chiefs in two special tepees. Then they took down their lodges and packed them up. A long stream of women, crying children, ponies, and barking dogs moved southward, guarded by lines of galloping warriors. The Indians headed toward the Bighorn Mountains. On the way, they divided into separate bands for safety.

A Terrible Discovery

On June 26, General Terry's troops were advancing southward. In the distance they saw some Indian scouts who signaled that the Seventh Cavalry had been defeated. The soldiers refused to believe that this was possible. The truth was soon obvious. When the soldiers stumbled onto the dreadful battlefield, they were stunned with horror.

Soon they reached Major Reno and his men, who were still searching for Custer's troops. They were in a state of shock and could not believe that Custer's column had been destroyed. Now the survivors faced a long journey eastward. Many of the wounded needed surgery or nursing, Some were still dazed.

Heroes and Villains

News of the Battle of Little Bighorn spread quickly throughout North America. The Indians knew about it long before the whites. Smoke signals could be faster than the newly invented telegraph, which often broke down.

Most white Americans thought Custer had been a great hero. Some soldiers disagreed and accused him of having been rash. Others blamed Reno for the defeat. However, the public had few doubts.

▼ *The Indians broke up their huge camp and rode to the mountains. For how long would they be safe from the Bluecoats?*

LITTLE BIGHORN

The newspapers demanded revenge for the defeat at Little Bighorn. The Indians would pay dearly for their victory. And so they did. Soon, soldiers were swarming over the Powder River country. This time, they had cannons and were well armed and supplied. The Sioux warriors were supposed to be brought in as prisoners of war, but many Cheyenne and Sioux were killed.

Defeat in Victory

The Indians had won a great victory over the Seventh Cavalry. They knew that it would be their last. They had run out of supplies and ammunition, and now the whole white nation had united against them.

Finally the Indians signed a treaty, giving up the Black Hills to the miners and settlers. Some Sioux warriors were given money to go to fight other Indian tribes farther to the west, such as the Nez Percé. Others were paid to act as police on the reservations.

▶ *The great Sioux chief Red Cloud had fought the Bluecoats for many years. Now he had to care for his people on the reservations where they were forced to live.*

The Ghost Dance

The Oglalas under Crazy Horse, along with a few other bands of Indians, continued their fight for a time. But in May 1877 the threat of starvation finally forced Crazy Horse to surrender at Fort Robinson. In September, the army feared he was planning to escape, and tried to imprison him. When Crazy Horse resisted, a soldier killed him with a bayonet thrust.

Sitting Bull had led his people across the border to Canada. The cavalry could not follow him into another country, but the Americans tried to persuade him to return. They offered him a full pardon. It was not until 1881 that he decided to return home and give himself up.

Sitting Bull became famous. This veteran warrior even joined a circus, touring with Buffalo Bill's Wild West Show. He signed his autograph for a few coins. Despite all this, Sitting Bull kept his pride and dignity. He continued to speak up for his people, as more land was taken from them.

▼ *In October 1877 the United States government sent soldiers to Canada to persuade Sitting Bull to return. He refused. He wished to stay in the "Land of the Grandmother." He meant Queen Victoria, for Canada was then a part of the British Empire. Sitting Bull said that the United States were "poisoned by blood." It was four years before he did return.*

LITTLE BIGHORN

Dancing for a Dream

In the late 1880s, many Indians on reservations began to perform a new kind of dance. They had strange visions in which Jesus Christ met with ancient Indian spirits. They believed their dancing and chanting would cause the return of the buffalo, their great warriors, and their old way of life — and the disappearance of the whites.

This Ghost Dance was very popular on Sitting Bull's reservation. The whites became nervous, and more soldiers were ordered into the reservation. On December 15, 1890, Sitting Bull was arrested and killed during a scuffle with Indians who were serving as police.

A few days later a similar scuffle broke out at a camp at Wounded Knee in South Dakota. Soldiers immediately opened fire on the chief, Bigfoot, and whole families around him. At least 153 Indians were **massacred** on the spot, and many more crawled away to die in the snow.

The Indian Wars ended at Wounded Knee. The white soldiers had not only stolen the rich lands of the Sioux and Cheyenne, they had taken the hunting grounds of the Nez Percé, the mountains of the Utes, the deserts and canyons of the Apaches. From the Atlantic to the Pacific Ocean, the whites now "owned" all the land they had wanted for so long.

United States Citizens

By 1924 all Indians had officially become citizens of the United States, but they were still treated very badly. For many years Hollywood films continued to depict the Indians as painted savages. Only the white people were shown to be brave or heroic.

Today, many American Indians are still poor. Some live on reservations, others in towns and cities. In their own land they are greatly outnumbered by people of other cultures. American Indians may face an uncertain future but they are increasingly determined to protect their remaining territories and their rights.

▶ *The Ghost Dancers believed that if they danced, the Indian warriors would rise from the dead. The hated Bluecoats would vanish from the earth and the buffalo would return. The dancers wore special shirts, which they believed gave them magical protection against bullets. At Wounded Knee they learned that this was not true.*

Glossary

allies: forces which unite to fight a common enemy

artillery: large guns, such as cannons, which are mounted on a carriage or a fixed base

buffalo: a name given to the North American bison, a large wild ox

campaign: the operations of an army in a region during a particular season

carbine: a short-barreled rifle suitable for use on horseback

cavalry: troops trained to fight on horseback

civilization: any society which has made great advances in science and the arts or in government. Great American Indian civilizations included those of the Aztecs in Mexico, the Mayans in Mexico and Central America, and the Incas in South America.

civil war: a war fought between people within a single country. The Civil War of 1861–1865 was fought between Union (northern) troops and Confederate (southern) troops.

column: a line of soldiers on the march

council: a meeting of the leading men of a tribe or band, called to discuss important matters such as war, hunting, or moving camp

coup stick: lance curved at the top like a shepherd's crook. The Plains Indians used it to strike a live enemy's body with a blow (in French, *coup*). This was considered to be an especially brave act.

desert: to leave an army without permission. Soldiers who deserted faced severe punishment, imprisonment, or even death.

discipline: a system of orders and rules which soldiers have to obey

guerrilla: in Spanish, this word means "little war." It describes a kind of fighting which relies on raids, ambushes, or sabotage to wear down the enemy.

Indians: a name given to Native Americans by the first European explorers. They thought they had arrived in southeast Asia, which was known as the Indies.

infantry: troops trained to fight on foot

lodge: any shelter used by the North American Indians. These varied from region to region. In the northwest, Indians built cedarwood houses. In the southwest, many lived in dwellings built into cliffs. The Plains Indians lived in tepees made of buffalo hide, which could be moved from one site to another.

massacre: to kill everyone, whether or not they are part of the fighting force, including women, children, old people, animals. Massacres of Indians occurred at Sand Creek and Wounded Knee.

medicine man: a name for a shaman, or spiritual leader of an Indian tribe. His dreams and visions were important to the whole tribe. He knew all the rituals, ceremonies, and traditions of his people.

Native Americans: the people who lived in the Americas before the arrival of the Europeans

Plains Wars: the series of wars made by the United States Army against Indian nations of the Great Plains, such as the Sioux and Cheyenne. The wars lasted from 1854 until 1890.

prairie: a broad, grassy plain. The North American prairies lie to the east of the Rocky Mountains, in the United States and Canada.

prospector: somebody who searches an area for minerals such as gold or silver

racism: the belief that one race of humans is superior to another

ranch: (from the Spanish *rancho*, "a farm") a farm where animals are reared

regiment: a unit of soldiers such as the Seventh Cavalry

LITTLE BIGHORN

reinforcements: extra troops who arrive to help a fighting force

reservation: an area of land reserved by the government for a particular group of American Indians. Many Indians still live on reservations.

revolver: a kind of handgun. It has a revolving cylinder with a number of chambers containing bullets. As the cylinder turns, it allows a number of bullets to be shot in succession before reloading.

saber: a heavy slashing sword used by cavalry. It is slightly curved and has only one sharp edge.

scalp: the skin at the top of the head, from which the hair grows

scout: a fighter who goes ahead of the main force in order to check out and report back on the lay of the land or the position of the enemy

sheath knife: a long, sharp knife traditionally used for fighting or hunting and strapped to the body in a leather sheath. Custer's men referred to them as "butcher knives."

skirmish: a minor fight between two armies or bands of warriors

smoke signals: a means of sending messages by a code of puffs of smoke. These could be produced by holding a blanket over a smoking fire.

telegraph: a method of sending coded messages by an electric instrument along a wire

tepee: a large conical tent made of buffalo hide draped over tall wooden poles. Three or four poles supported the main weight and then others were added for extra strength.

territory: a large area of land which is not recognized as a country in its own right

tomahawk: a wooden club inset with a sharp cutting blade, used by American Indians

travois: (from the French travail, "travel") a frame of two poles with packs tied to them. They were dragged behind dogs or horses.

treaty: a formal agreement between different nations

tribes: a name given to different nations, or groups, of Indians

veteran: a soldier with experience of battle

wickiup: temporary shelter made of branches by Indian warriors or hunters

Further Reading

Black, Sheila. *Sitting Bull*. New Jersey: Silver Burdett, 1989.

Chief Joseph's Own Story As Told By Chief Joseph in 1879. Billings, Montana: Council for Indian Education, 1972.

Fichter, George. *How the Plains Indians Lived*. New York: McKay, 1980.

Halliburton, Warren J. *The Tragedy of Little Bighorn*. New York: Franklin Watts, 1989.

Kent, Zachary. *The Story of Geronimo*. Chicago: Children's Press, 1989.

Marrin, Albert. *War Clouds in the West: Indians and Cavalrymen, 1860–1890*. New York: Atheneum, 1984.

McGraw, Jessie B. *Chief Red Horse Tells About Custer*. New York: Lodestar, 1981.

Razzi, Jim. *Custer and Crazy Horse*. New York: Scholastic, 1989.

Shorto, Russell. *Geronimo*. New Jersey: Silver Burdett, 1989.

Stein, R. Conrad. *The Story of Little Bighorn*. Chicago: Children's Press, 1989.

Index

PRINTED IN BELGIUM BY

INTERNATIONAL BOOK PRODUCTION